Dinosaurs Alive!

Iguanodon

and other plant-eating dinosaurs

Jinny Johnson

Illustrated by Graham Rosewarne

FRANKLIN WATTS
LONDON•SYDNEY

An Appleseed Editions book

First published in 2007 by Franklin Watts

Franklin Watts
338 Euston Road, London NW1 3BH

Franklin Watts Australia
Hachette Children's Books
Level 17/207 Kent St, Sydney, NSW 2000

© 2007 Appleseed Editions

Created by Appleseed Editions Ltd,
Well House, Friars Hill, Guestling,
East Sussex TN35 4ET

Designed by Helen James
Edited by Mary-Jane Wilkins
Artwork by Graham Rosewarne

ISBN 978 07496 7544 8

Dewey Classification: 567.914

A CIP catalogue for this book is available from the British Library

Photographs by
Science Photo Library page 28
Mehau Kulyk/Science Photo Library page 29

Printed in China

Franklin Watts is a division of Hachette Children's Books

Contents

Dinosaurs' world

A dinosaur was a kind of reptile that lived millions of years ago. Dinosaurs lived long before there were people on Earth.

We know about dinosaurs because many of their bones and teeth have been discovered. Scientists called palaeontologists (pay-lee-on-tol-ojists) learn a lot about the animals by studying these bones.

The first dinosaurs lived about 225 million years ago. They disappeared – became extinct – about 65 million years ago. Some scientists believe that birds are a type of dinosaur so they say there are still dinosaurs living all around us!

Scutellosaurus

TRIASSIC
248 to 205 million years ago
Dinosaurs that lived at this time include:
Coelophysis, Eoraptor, Liliensternus, Plateosaurus,
Riojasaurus, Saltopus

EARLY JURASSIC
205 to 180 million years ago
Dinosaurs that lived at this time include:
Crylophosaurus, Dilophosaurus, Lesothosaurus,
Massospondylus, Scelidosaurus, Scutellosaurus

Lesothosaurus

LATE JURASSIC
180 to 144 million years ago
Dinosaurs that lived at this time include:
Allosaurus, Apatosaurus, Brachiosaurus,
Ornitholestes, Stegosaurus, Yangchuanosaurus

EARLY CRETACEOUS
144 to 98 million years ago
Dinosaurs that lived at this time include: Baryonyx,
Giganotosaurus, Iguanodon, Leaellynasaura,
Muttaburrasaurus, Nodosaurus, Sauropelta

LATE CRETACEOUS
98 to 65 million years ago
Dinosaurs that lived at this time include:
Ankylosaurus, Gallimimus, Maiasaura, Triceratops,
Tyrannosaurus, Velociraptor

Velociraptor

Iguanodon

Iguanodon was one of the first dinosaurs ever to be discovered and named, in 1822. Scientists thought the fossilized teeth looked like a giant iguana lizard's, so called it Iguanodon.

IGUANODON

Group: ornithopods (iguanodonts)

Length: up to 10 metres

Lived in: Europe, North America

When: Early Cretaceous, 140-110 million years ago

This is how you say
Iguanodon:
Ig-wah-noh-don

Huge herds of Iguanodon roamed
forests during the Early Cretaceous.
They fed on all sorts of plants,
which they chewed with
their strong flat teeth.

An Iguanodon probably
ate about 130 kilograms
of plant food every day.
That's like eating
150 lettuces,
90 cucumbers
and 300 apples.

*Iguanodon moved
on all fours, but
may have reared
up on its back
legs to feed
or to scare off
an enemy.*

7

Inside Iguanodon

Big strong bones supported Iguanodon's bulky body. The dinosaur had a long skull with a sharp beak at the front of its jaws for chopping mouthfuls of plants.

Dinosaurs lived long before there were people on Earth. But here you can see how big a dinosaur would look compared with a seven-year-old child.

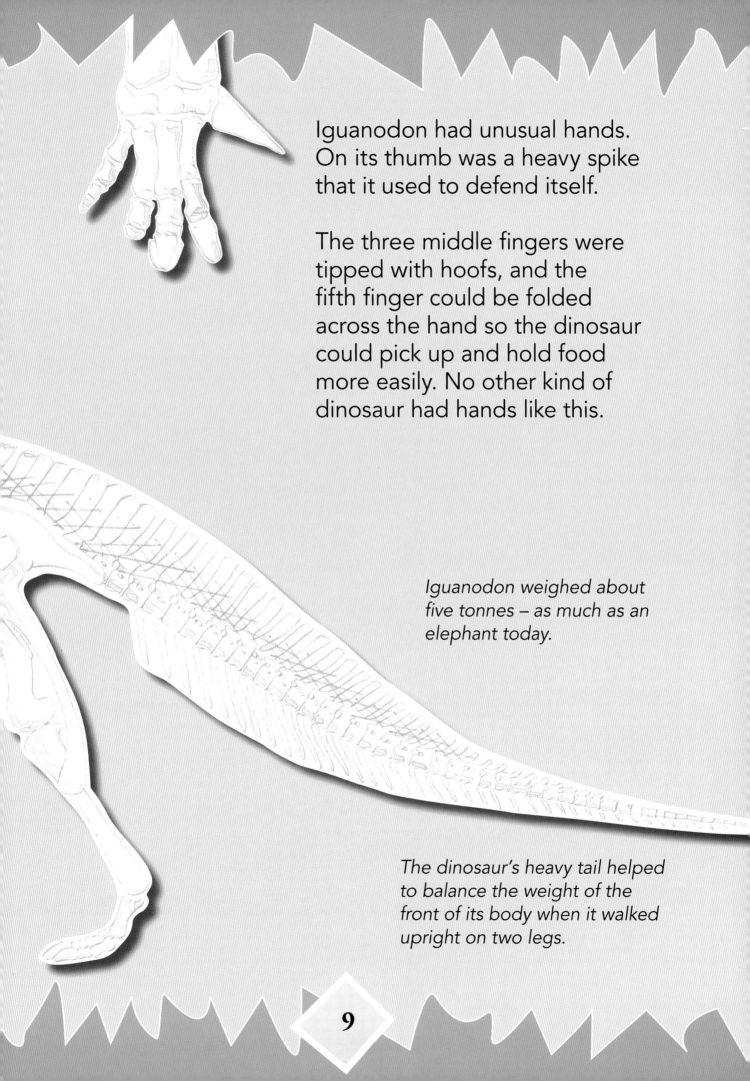

Iguanodon had unusual hands. On its thumb was a heavy spike that it used to defend itself.

The three middle fingers were tipped with hoofs, and the fifth finger could be folded across the hand so the dinosaur could pick up and hold food more easily. No other kind of dinosaur had hands like this.

Iguanodon weighed about five tonnes – as much as an elephant today.

The dinosaur's heavy tail helped to balance the weight of the front of its body when it walked upright on two legs.

Iguanodon in action

Iguanodon was often attacked by predatory dinosaurs, like all plant-eaters. It defended itself with its thumb spikes.

Most of the time Iguanodon moved peacefully around in herds as it searched for plants to eat.

Living in herds helped to protect younger, weaker animals against attacks. Iguanodons could probably move at 15-20 kilometres an hour, running at full speed. When threatened, Iguanodon reared up on its back legs and jabbed its attacker with the sharp spike.

Iguanodon could deal a deadly blow with its thumb spike, driving it deep into its attacker's flesh.

Ouranosaurus

This relative of Iguanodon was
a smaller dinosaur with a longer head.
It had two little bumps on its snout.

Ouranosaurus had a row of tall bones sticking up
from its backbone which were probably covered
with skin so they looked like a sail. This may have
helped to control its body temperature.

When Ouranosaurus wanted to warm up it turned
the sail into the sun so the blood flowing through
the sail skin heated up. To cool down, it turned
away from the sun.

This is how you say
Ouranosaurus:
Ooh-rah-noh-sore-us

OURANOSAURUS

Group: ornithopods (iguanodonts)

Length: up to 7 metres

Lived in: West Africa

When: Early Cretaceous, 115-100 million years ago

Ouranosaurus's sail may have helped the dinosaur scare off enemies, or it might have attracted a mate.

Muttaburrasaurus

Muttaburrasaurus probably looked
very like Iguanodon, with spikes on its thumbs.
It had very strong jaws and sharp teeth for biting
off mouthfuls of tough plants.

This dinosaur had a larger snout than Iguanodon
and it was topped with a big bony bump. This
may have helped to make its calls louder. The
dinosaur also had very big nostrils which might
have given it an extra good sense of smell and
so helped it find food.

This is how you say
Muttaburrasaurus:
Mut-a-burra-sore-us

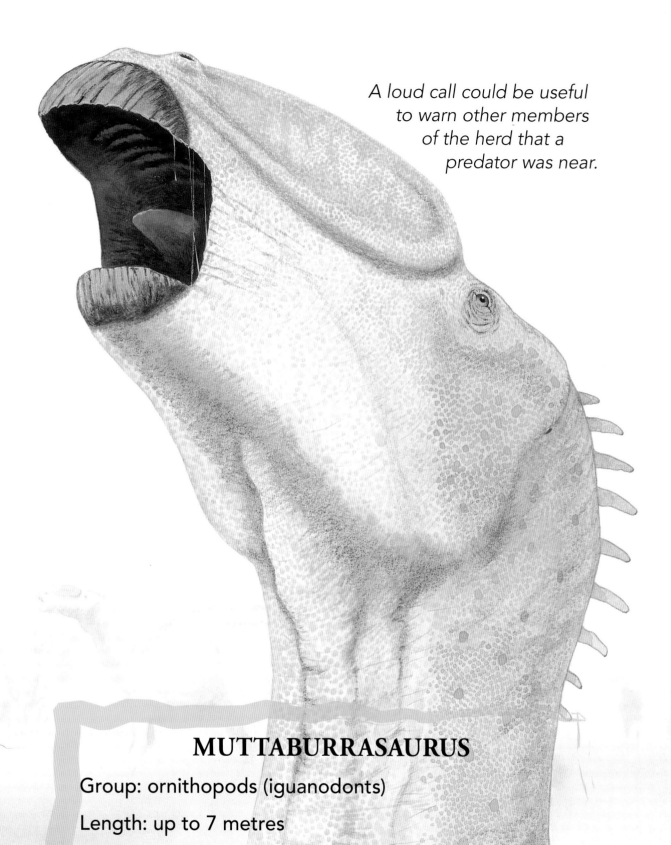

A loud call could be useful to warn other members of the herd that a predator was near.

MUTTABURRASAURUS

Group: ornithopods (iguanodonts)

Length: up to 7 metres

Lived in: Australia

When: Early Cretaceous, 110-100 million years ago

Leaellynasaura

These small dinosaurs wandered the forests eating low-growing plants, as herds of deer do today. They walked upright, but could scurry about on all fours when feeding.

Leaellynasaura lived in the south of Australia, which at that time was part of the Antarctic. This area was not quite as freezing then as it is now, but winters would have been very cold and dark.

Leaellynasaura could probably run fast on its long, slender back legs.

LEAELLYNASAURA

Group: ornithopods (hypsilophodonts)

Length: up to 2 metres

Lived in: Australia

When: Early Cretaceous, 115-110 million years ago

This is how you say
Leaellynasaura:
Lee-ell-ina-sore-a

Fossil bones show that Leaellynasaura had very large eyes which may have helped it to see in the dim light of the Antarctic winter. In summer it probably spent all day and night feeding, so it could build up fat to survive the winter.

Fabrosaurs

Fabrosaurs, such as Lesothosaurus and Scutellosaurus, were plant-eaters about the size of a fox or badger today. They gathered plant food with their narrow jaws and sharp, pointed teeth, and may have lived in burrows underground.

This is how you say Lesothosaurus: Le-so-toe-sore-us

LESOTHOSAURUS

Group: ornithopods (fabrosaurs)

Length: up to 1 metre

Lived in: Africa

When: Early Jurassic, 213-200 million years ago

SCUTELLOSAURUS

Group: ornithopods (fabrosaurs)

Length: up to 1.2 metres

Lived in: western North America

When: Early Jurassic, 205-202 million years ago

This is how you say
Scutellosaurus:
Skoo-tel-oh-sore-us

These little plant-eaters probably did not live in herds like larger dinosaurs, but scurried around on their own, looking for food.

Fabrosaurs moved fast on their long back legs. They had no sharp claws to defend themselves so could only run away from predators. Scutellosaurus had some bony plates covering its back, which may have helped to protect it from attackers.

Heterodontosaurus

This little dinosaur was a plant-eater, but it had unusual teeth. Unlike most other plant-eating dinosaurs, it had three sorts of teeth, shaped for different tasks.

At the front of its jaws were sharp, pointed teeth for cutting leaves. Further back were larger teeth for chewing. Heterodontosaurus also had two pairs of long teeth that looked like a dog's teeth. This was very unusual for a plant-eating dinosaur.

Probably only the male Heterodontosaurus had tusk-like teeth. It may have used them to fight rivals for mates during the breeding season.

HETERODONTOSAURUS

Group: ornithopods (heterodontosaurs)

Length: up to 1.2 metres

Lived in: southern Africa

When: Early Jurassic, 205 million years ago

This is how you say
Heterodontosaurus:
Het-er-oh-dont-oh-sore-us

Maiasaura

Hadrosaurs, such as Maiasaura, were some of the most common dinosaurs during the Late Cretaceous.

These dinosaurs are also known as duckbills because they had a long flat beak at the front of the mouth.

Maiasaura lived in herds. It probably walked on four legs when feeding but could rear up on two legs to flee from danger.

MAIASAURA

Group: ornithopods (hadrosaurs)

Length: up to 9 metres

Lived in: North America

When: Late Cretaceous, 80-75 million years ago

Maiasaura cropped plants with its toothless beak and then chewed using the teeth further back in its mouth. It had a very flexible neck, so it could bend and reach for food without moving around much.

This is how you say Maiasaura:
My-ah-sore-ah

Good mother lizard

The name Maiasaura means good mother lizard. Fossils have been found of Maiasaura's nests, eggs and young.

The Maiasaura mother laid her eggs in layers in a hollow in the ground. She covered each layer with earth and topped the nest with more earth to hide the eggs from other dinosaurs.

Each egg was about 18 centimetres long – about three times the size of a chicken's egg. The mother probably lay by the nest to protect the eggs.

A dinosaur egg had a tough waterproof shell to protect the young inside.

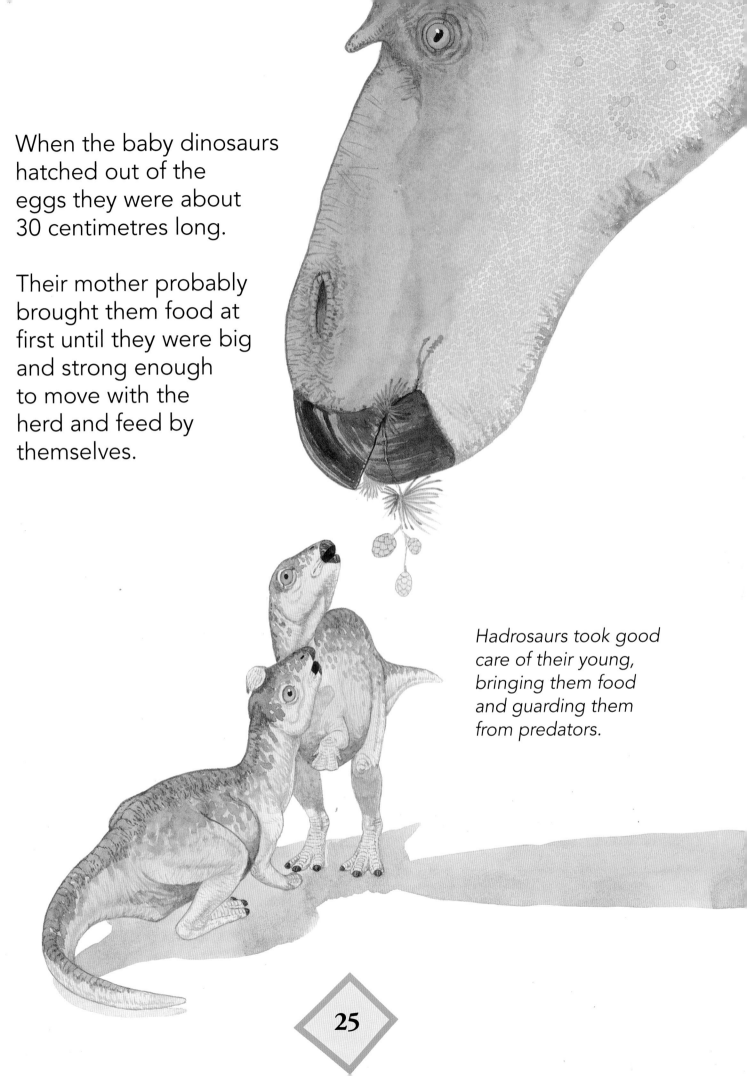

When the baby dinosaurs hatched out of the eggs they were about 30 centimetres long.

Their mother probably brought them food at first until they were big and strong enough to move with the herd and feed by themselves.

Hadrosaurs took good care of their young, bringing them food and guarding them from predators.

Crested duckbills

Many kinds of duckbill dinosaurs had a large crest on top of their heads.

Some crests were spikes, but Lambeosaurus had a rounded crest like a helmet. Parasaurolophus's crest was as long as the body of an adult human.

This is how you say Lambeosaurus:
Lam-bee-oh-sore-us

LAMBEOSAURUS

Group: ornithopods (hadrosaurs)

Length: up to 9 metres

Lived in: Canada

When: Late Cretaceous, 76-74 million years ago

The crests were hollow inside and they may have made the dinosaurs' roaring calls louder. The calls helped the animals in a herd keep in touch with each other and find mates.

Every type of duckbill had a different call and they could recognize the calls of their own kind.

PARASAUROLOPHUS

Group: ornithopods
(hadrosaurs)

Length: up to 11 metres

Lived in: North America

When: Late Cretaceous,
76-74 million years ago

This is how you say
Parasaurolophus:
Pa-ra-saw-rol-off-us

27

Who discovered dinosaurs?

In 1822 a British doctor called Dr Mantell and his wife Mary found some strange teeth as they walked in the country.

When he looked closely at the teeth, Dr Mantell realized they were like reptile teeth. He thought they might have belonged to a giant iguana (a kind of lizard).

Twenty years later a scientist called Richard Owen realized that these teeth and other fossilized teeth and bones that had been found, belonged to a special group of reptiles. He called them dinosaurs, which means 'terrible lizards'.

Since then the remains of dinosaurs have been found all over the world. We now know there were at least 700 different kinds.

Gideon Mantell was one of the first people to find dinosaur fossils.

An Iguanodon skeleton in a museum in 1883. When the first Iguanodon skeletons were put together the thumb spike was placed on the dinosaur's nose, like a horn.

Words to remember

Antarctica
The area around the South Pole.

crest
A bony shape on a dinosaur's head.

duckbill dinosaurs
Dinosaurs with a long flattened beak, like a duck's beak, at the front of the jaws. Lambeosaurus was a duckbill dinosaur.

fabrosaur
A small, fast-moving dinosaur which fed on plants. Lesothosaurus was a fabrosaur.

fossils
Parts of an animal such as bones and teeth that have been preserved in rock over millions of years.

iguana
A kind of lizard. Some iguanas grow to two metres long.

ornithopod
Ornithopods were a group of plant-eating dinosaurs which included iguanodonts, hadrosaurs and fabrosaurs. They lived during the Jurassic and Cretaceous periods.

palaeontologist
A scientist who looks for and studies fossils to find out more about the creatures of the past.

plates
Extra pieces of bone on the body of some dinosaurs.

predator
An animal that hunts and kills other animals.

reptile
An animal with a backbone and a dry scaly body. Most reptiles lay eggs with leathery shells. Dinosaurs were reptiles. Today's reptiles include lizards, snakes, turtles and crocodiles.

sail
A structure on the back of some types of dinosaur. The sail was made of tall bones sticking up from the dinosaur's back and covered with skin.

Index